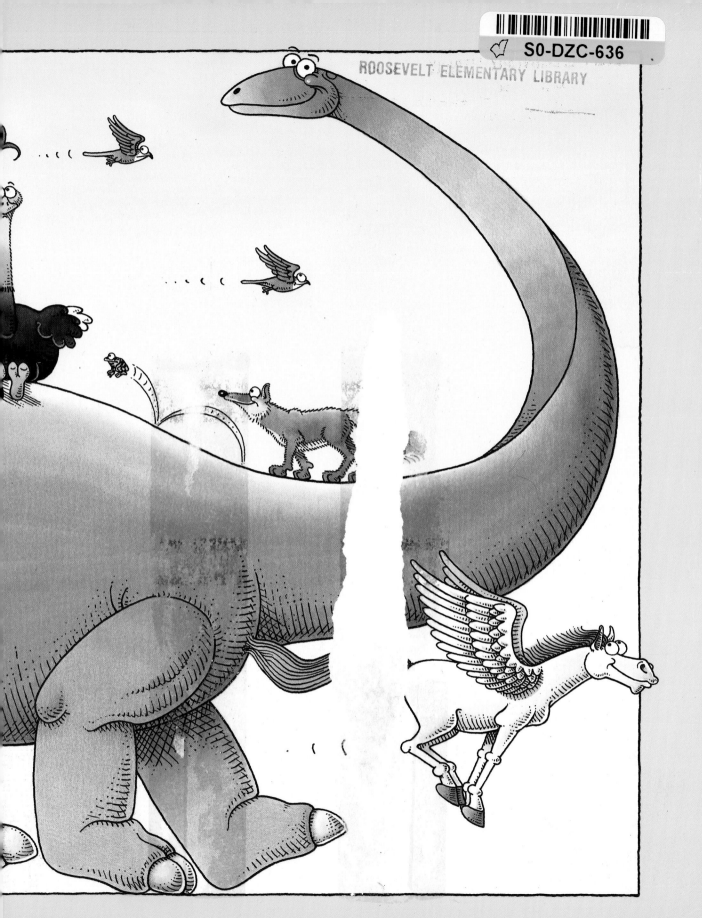

For Poppaea from S.G.

For Sarahjane from M.E.

A TRELD BICKNELL BOOK

Published by Whispering Coyote Press, Inc.
480 Newbury Street, Suite 104, Danvers,
Massachusetts 01923

Printed in Hong Kong for Imago Publishing

10 9 8 7 6 5 4 3 2 1

Library of Congress Cataloging-in-Publication Data

Greenway, Shirley
   Dragons, dolphins, & dinosaurs (wacky
facts about animals)/compiled by Shirley
Greenway: illustrated by Michael Evans.
        p.   c.

   Includes index:
   Summary: A compilation of facts about
unusual animals, arranged in such
categories as "Animal Extemes," "Funny
Fish," and "Hide and Seek."

ISBN: 1-879085-83-6

1. Animals miscellanae—juvenile
literature. (1. Animals-Miscellanea.)
I. Evans, Michael, 1966- ill.   II. Title

QL49.G755 1993   93-20397
591-dc20   CIP
                                        AC

Dragons, Dolphins, and Dinosaurs

Wacky Facts About Animals

Compiled by

SHIRLEY GREENWAY

Illustrated by

MICHAEL EVANS

Whispering Coyote Press, Inc./Boston

Contents

1. A World of Giants 　　　　　　　　7

2. Animal Extremes 　　　　　　　　10

3. Here Be Dragons! 　　　　　　　　14

4. It Takes All Kinds 　　　　　　　　18

5. Funny Fish 　　　　　　　　　　22

6. Hide and Seek 　　　　　　　　24

7. How The Other Half Lives 　　　　26

　Animal Index 　　　　　　　　　30

1. A World of Giants

Millions of years ago the world was ruled by animals. Monstrous reptiles roamed the earth feeding on its rich vegetation and were in turn preyed upon by terrifying flesh-eating dinosaurs. The largest of these "terrible lizards" grew to a colossal size. The giant plant-eaters like the **Brontosaurus**, **Brachiosaurus**, and **Diplodocus** were *the largest animals ever to live on land*.

* **Diplodocus** ("double beam") was one of the longest. Skeletons found in Utah 80 years ago gave scientists the first clues to just how *big* these giant reptiles were. They calculated that the slow-moving vegetarian Diplodocus was more than 87 feet long, stood almost 12 feet high, and weighed more than 10 tons. To help them digest the rough vegetation that was their only food, these huge sauropods first swallowed rocks—to create their own internal grinding machines!

* But Diplodocus was a lightweight compared with the massive **Brachiosaurus**. Called the "arm-lizard," this enormous beast grew to more than 20 feet in height and weighed more than 75 tons—as much as 8 Diplodocuses and more than 14 elephants!

North America was obviously a favorite haunt of dinosaurs over 100 million years ago, for more fossil bones have been found there than in any other place on earth. New finds are still being made and the bones of bigger and bigger animals found —suggesting that the very biggest of all the dinosaurs may have been one-and-half times as long as Diplodocus and twice as heavy as Brachiosaurus—making it truly a "seismosaurus" or earth-shaker!

* **Tyrannosaurus Rex** also lived in North America, 75 million years ago. This infamous "Tyrant Lizard" was not as heavy as the ponderous plant-eating animals it hunted—and bigger flesh-eating dinosaurs existed even then—but *none* seems to have surpassed T. Rex for sheer ferocity!

* The poor old **Stegasaurus** wasn't very smart, with a tiny brain weighing only $2\frac{1}{2}$ ounces. But, luckily, this small brain didn't have to do *all* the work, because Stegasaurus, had separate nerve centers (20 times larger than its brain) which "automatically" controlled the movement of its massive legs and tail!

* The **Pteranodon** was a prehistoric flying reptile, with an enormous wingspan of more than 27 feet. Its arms had become wings, its bones were hollow (like those of birds), and its trailing legs were too weak for walking —Pteranodon had become a "flying machine". The **Pterosaur** was a glider which launched itself on a brisk wind and—like the heavy huge-winged **albatross**—simply stayed aloft for days.

* **Archaeopteryx** was half-reptile and half-bird. It had sharp teeth and a long tail like its ancestors the giant reptiles, but was the *first creature to have feathers*, like its descendants, the birds.

* The tusks of an adult **woolly mammoth** were more than 16 feet long!

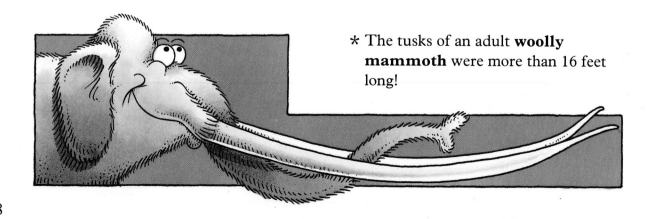

* The world's first professional fossil hunter was a young girl called Mary Anning. She lived in Lyme Regis, a small town on the south coast of England. The cliffs of Lyme were stuffed with fossil remains and in 1812 Mary Anning made a stunning discovery: the complete 17-foot skeleton of a prehistoric sea creature —**Ichthyosaur**. At the time it was 180 million years old; Mary Anning was only 12!

* That fearsome reptile, the **crocodile**, has been around for about 75 million years! The salt-water croc is still the world's largest reptile—the only reminder of what its huge ancestors must have looked like. But the biggest crocodile on record is only half as long as the original **Phobosuchus**—the "horror crocodile!"

* Reptiles *did* fly in prehistoric time but some of the very earliest of early birds did not. The **elephant bird** of Madagascar—the fabled "**Roc**" of the Arabian Nights—was 10 feet tall and weighed 1,000 pounds. Not surprisngly, it couldn't fly. The Roc did, however, lay huge and wonderful eggs. The elephant bird's egg was larger than a dinosaur egg—and seven times the size of an ostrich egg, the largest laid by any bird now alive.

9

2. Animal Extremes

* Only one animal now exists which is larger than its prehistoric ancestors —the mighty **whale**. The whales which swam the southern seas 38 million years ago were certainly very big, measuring 60-70 feet in length. But the female **blue whale**—*the world's largest animal*—can grow to be

* **Blue whales** can move surprisingly fast for such ponderous animals. Moving swiftly through the water, a blue whale can—luckily—outrun a whaling ship, *and stay ahead of it all day*. It's no wonder Captain Ahab had such trouble hunting down the famous *Moby Dick!*

more than 100 feet long, and weighs as much as the heaviest dinosaur.

* **African elephants** have to carry their own great weight on land, but at $5\frac{1}{2}$ tons that is quite a lot to carry as they move in stately procession through the bush. *The largest living land animals,* the tallest elephants stand more than 12 feet high. Better still, when standing on tiptoe with trunk out-stretched, an elephant can reach branches that would be too high for a giraffe!

* **Giraffes**, on the other hand, don't need to stand on tiptoe. When you are 18 feet tall, you can generally eat all the sun-drenched leaves that other animals can't reach.

Coyote outwitted?

Have you ever wondered whether the **roadrunner** could really get away from the **coyote** every time? Certainly this odd bird seems to like being chased and, when it gets its stride, the roadrunner can zip along at more than 25 miles an hour.

It is said that a horseman once spotted one of these long-tailed birds standing in the middle of the road, about 300 feet ahead of him. He decided to test its speed and gave chase. The roadrunner promptly took up the challenge and, with neck outstretched and wings extended as stabilisers, off it ran. It *could* simply have flown away but actually prefers to run!

It screamed along the dead straight road—as if the coyote were in hot pursuit—for a quarter of a mile before diving into a thicket, leaving the galloping horseman 150 feet behind!

* But what about the **coyote**? Well, in real life the wily coyote would have no trouble catching its prey—because its top speed is a road-burning 35 miles an hour! The scrawny roadrunner hardly seems worth the exercise, but a hungry coyote will eat just about anything.

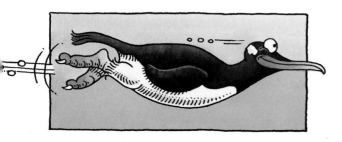

* The **Gentoo penguin** is as fast in the water as the roadrunner on a long straight road—swimming, at 25 miles an hour, *faster than any other bird.*

* Head in the sand? Not me!

But the fastest running bird is also the largest. The **ostrich** is *much* too heavy to fly but its huge muscular legs give it an excellent turn of speed. It can gallop along at more than 30 miles an hour for up to 20 minutes before tiring—and even more if it is frightened! This ought to keep ostriches safe from most predators but they have the strange habit of running in circles, which really works against them. Pursuing hunters can run across the diameter of the circle made by their quarry—or simply wait until the big bird comes around again!

This may leave the ostrich open to speculation about its intelligence, but one thing *is* certain—they do not bury their heads in the sand when danger threatens. Instead, being immensely strong, fast, and unbelievably bad-tempered—especially during the mating season—an ostrich will turn and fight. And it usually wins!

Ostriches swallow pebbles to help them digest their food, but if no pebbles are around, lots of other things will do—from spoons, padlocks, coins, keys, and tools to pocket watches and even uncut diamonds!

* YY-aa-aa-aa-www-www-nnn!

It is so slow being a sloth. The tropical **three-toed sloth** travels at a careful 6-8 feet per minute (.07 miles an hour), but up in the trees the sloth can really move—more than doubling its speed on the ground—especially when it gets warmed up!

* *Speed on the wing . . .*

Birds can travel faster than any other animals, but most birds can't fly any faster than the normal highway speed limit—between 50-60 miles an hour.

One bird which really exceeds the limit, however, is the **Asian spine-tailed swift**. Soaring aloft on their sickle-shaped wings, these small flying aces have been timed at airspeeds—the speed which it flies in relation to the air rather than the ground—of more than 100 miles per hour. *It's no wonder that they are the fastest things in the air not piloting an airplane!*

* *A moggy menace . . .*

Lions have the reputation of being efficient hunters, and **tigers** are the biggest, fiercest, and stealthiest of all the big cats—but the real champion hunter of the feline world is the well-fed domestic pussycat!

* The wings of the tiny **hummingbird** beat so fast as it hovers to feed that they become no more than a blur of bright color and a long hh-uu-uu-mm-mm!

Of course, some cats have official jobs—there are good "ratters" on farms and in railroad stations, post offices, and factories. Worthy cats all! But it seems that when house cats go out at night they are responsible for the deaths of millions of small mammals and birds—70 million in cat-loving Britain every year!

* 35,000 **kittens** are born in America every day—that is, *three kittens for every human baby.*

* *Fly sprays at the ready . . .*

The **common housefly** is the carrier of more than thirty different diseases —including some of the worst: cholera, bubonic plague, leprosy, and smallpox —*making the fly more dangerous to humans than any other animal in history.*

* But nothing can compare with **humans** themselves—*the most powerful, destructive, and deadly animals ever to live on Earth*. Humans have been responsible for the destruction of untold numbers of individual animals, as well as the total extinction of many different types of the world's other animal inhabitants.

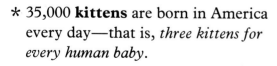

3. Here Be Dragons!

From ancient times animals have played a central part in the mythology of peoples from every part of the world. For some, animals symbolized the elements of nature —earth, sun, wind, and sky—for others, they were agents of gods in the creation of the world. Often the gods themselves were represented in animal forms.

Greek mythology is full of stories of gods and heroes facing tests of strength and cunning against terrible animal monsters or fighting for glory at the side of a brave beast. Some of them were fictional versions of real animals—like **Cerberus** the three-headed hound set to guard the entrance to the underworld, or **Pegasus**, the great winged horse who was the companion of the hero Bellerophon.

But the really wonderful monsters were created from parts of *several* animals. There were horrible ones like the **Chimera**—which was part goat, part lion; with the tail of a venomous snake. There were also noble ones like the **Griffin**. It was the offspring of a lion and an eagle—two of nature's finest creatures. The Griffin was sacred to the sun and became an emblem of valor.

Animals like **lions**, **eagles**, **falcons**, **bulls**, and **wolves** represented strength, honesty, nobility, and truth; while **snakes**, **lizards**, and the great creatures of the sea became symbols of terror, evil, and nightmare.

The mysteries of the deep . . .

In the days when people believed that the earth was flat and many ships sailed away on the uncharted seas never to return, map-makers showed the great oceans filled with whirlpools, winds, and huge sea-monsters.

Sea journeys were truly voyages into the unknown and sailors a brave, but superstitious, band of adventurers. Their tales were filled with exotic lands, strange people, and fabulous beasts in which they *almost* believed . . .

It was said that a ship might run aground on an island that wasn't an island, and that a huge many-armed monster might reach out of the deep to pull a sailing ship beneath the waves!

* *Perhaps they were right.* The first sight of a gigantic **blue whale** or a 70-ton **whale shark**—*the world's largest fish*—would certainly stun the watching sailors, and deserve the description "sea-monster" in their reports.

Imagine a night of storm and howling winds, when suddenly the writhing tentacles of a **giant octopus** emerge from the dark seas—pale, suckered, and 30 feet long—its huge round eyes glittering in the eerie light of St. Elmo's fire dancing in the rigging.

* There were gentler tales as well—of smooth-skinned **mermaids** with shining green hair beckoning to homesick sailors. But, sadly, the lovely mermaids always disappeared if ships drew near, especially in warm shallow waters where the sea-cows play. The pale female **sea-cows** (**dugongs**), with their smooth skin, large tender eyes, and forked tails, shelter their young with a protective flipper in a very human way and like to play with them in the rolling waves. Alas, these 10-foot sea mammals have no shining green hair—merely a few green seaweed fronds on which they graze.

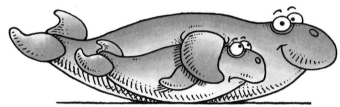

The Unique Unicorn . . .

Perhaps the most elusive of all mythological creatures was the **unicorn**—a gentle, hoofed animal with a single spiraling horn in the center of its forehead. The unicorn is often depicted as a small white **horse** with a **goat's** beard, a flowing mane, a **lion's** tail, and cloven hooves—clearly seen in the famous 15th century tapestry, *The Lady and the Unicorn.*

Its legend dates back thousands of years and stories of the virtuous unicorn have appeared all over the world. No-one knew exactly what the unicorn was—**horse, gazelle, goat, bull** or **rhinoceros**—but all the stories mentioned its purity and its single magic horn, which could make poison harmless. *It was much prized by royal households as a means of insuring the safety of their food.*

But was there ever a real unicorn?

* The **rhinoceros** has only one short horn, but this ponderous, bad-tempered beast hardly seems the right model for the sweet and graceful unicorn. But it, too is hunted for its "magical" horn.

However there once lived beautiful white-skinned **oxen**, called **aurochs**, which were hunted by the ancient kings of Babylon, where the legend began, 6000 years ago. Their long, curving horns were so perfectly placed that, seen from the side, they merged into one horn—and so they appear in the great carved hunting scenes which survive. Alas, the auroch *didn't* survive —it was hunted to extinction.

* One unique, spiral-horned animal *does* exist. In the icy northern seas lives another wonderfully strange sea creature—the **narwhal**. This small, shy whale sports a 10-foot long ivory tooth growing straight through its upper lip. Sold to those fearful European princes, the horn of the "unicorn of the sea" fueled the fantasy of the legendary white horse whose horn could cure almost anything, and keep them safe from their enemies. Fabulous prices were paid in medieval Europe for "unicorn horn" and, in 1982—*long after the narwhal itself was known as its true source*—the horn was sold for $400 per pound. Somewhere, someone will always believe in the magic of unicorns.

* *And then there were dragons!*
Like the unicorn the **dragon** is an ancient symbol—of wickedness. Part **serpent**, part **crocodile**, with huge teeth and fiery breath, dragons flew on great leathery wings. They were the guardians of treasure and captive princesses, and many a true hero lost his life in battle before a dragon was conquered.

But dragons take many forms: the beautiful five-clawed dragons of China represent wisdom; the image of the fire-breathing dragon on the prow of a swift Viking warship meant strength and success in battle; the red dragon of Wales is the proud symbol of princes.

Medieval European artists created a fantasy monster which looked very like the real lizards of nature—*creatures which they could never have seen in life!*

* The large **marine iguanas** of the Galapagos Islands have high-standing crests, cold eyes, spiked claws, and colorful overlapping scales—like so many medieval paintings of dragons.

* St. George is the most famous slayer of dragons, but is always shown putting to the sword a creature smaller than the average monster of myth. It looks, in fact, rather like the largest existing lizard, the aptly-named **Komodo dragon**. The Komodo is large (10 feet long) scaly, powerful, flesh-eating, and aggressive—a perfect candidate for

real-life dragon. But how did St. George ever meet one? Komodos are only found on a few small islands in Indonesia!

* The **Gila monster** of Arizona is a smaller desert lizard. It shares with the dragon a fondness for earth mounds and has a nasty, poisonous bite.

* Australia's **frilled lizard** is the most unusual, beautiful, and dragon-like of all lizards. When it gets angry, this yard-long "dragon" stands on its hind legs, unfurls the great ridged frill around its neck, and rushes the enemy—hissing loudly!

* *If looks could kill . . .*

The mythological **Basilisk** was a fearsome scaly lizard—the King of the Serpents. One look from the eye of the Basilisk meant certain death.

But the real **basilisk lizard** of Central America is a small harmless creature with beautiful bright green scales. *It can't kill with a look, but it can walk—or run—on water without sinking!*

4. It Takes All Kinds . . .

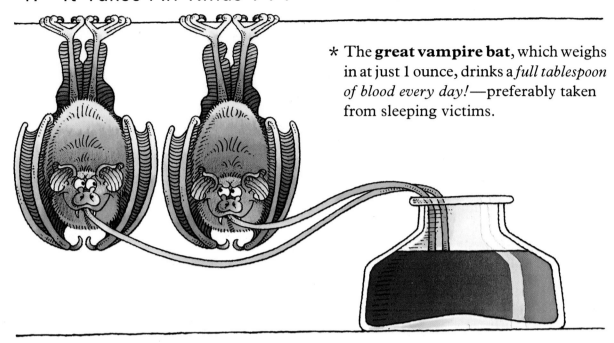

* The **great vampire bat**, which weighs in at just 1 ounce, drinks a *full tablespoon of blood every day!*—preferably taken from sleeping victims.

* *Shake a leg . . . or a tail!*

Crabs and **lobsters** have an ingenious way of getting themselves out of trouble. They can break off a trapped or damaged limb and grow a new one. **Lizards** can do the same with their tails (which are designed by nature to break off at a crucial joint) leaving predators with a mouthful of tail—but no lizard!

Sometimes the tail goes on wriggling long after it has been left behind—to keep the hungry hunter from chasing its tailless prey.

* The tiny and beautiful **arrow-poison frogs** from Central America secrete a poison so powerful that it can cause *instant* death—especially when delivered on the point of an Indian arrowhead.

* *How about a hug . . .*

Pythons are among the world's longest and heaviest snakes, but they can kill even bigger animals for their infrequent meals—*by squeezing them to death.*

* *Flying fur . . .*

Both the **flying squirrels** of North America and the **gliding possums** of Australia have found the perfect way to propel their small, furry bodies through their home forests. With legs spread wide the loose skin on their sides creates a useful parachute which carries them safely across the open spaces between the tall trees. They glide like soft shadows through the night —landing with a plop in the branches of another tree.

Flying squirrels are silent flyers, but the gliding possums—especially the sugar gliders—yell, snarl, scream, and whirr like stalled motors on a winter morning.

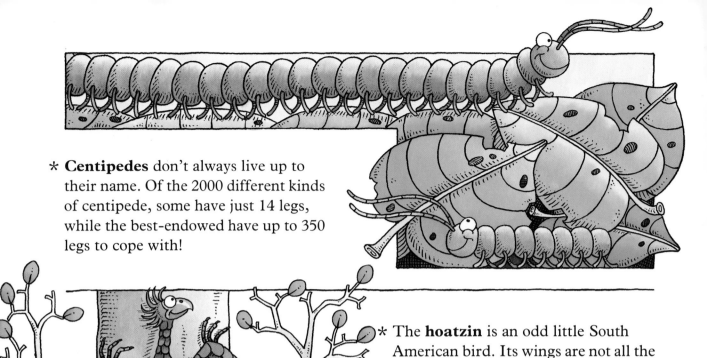

* **Centipedes** don't always live up to their name. Of the 2000 different kinds of centipede, some have just 14 legs, while the best-endowed have up to 350 legs to cope with!

* The **hoatzin** is an odd little South American bird. Its wings are not all the helpful for flying but, with claws along the edge of each wing, they can climb at great speed through the trees.

  Hoatzins look like miniature versions of **Archaeopteryx**—the world's first bird.

* **Axolotls** are amphibians with a very interesting life history! They live in the waters of a few lakes in Mexico and begin to lay eggs when they are still in their own "tadpole" form. When the lakes dry up—as they frequently do —the axolotls grow up, become adult salamanders, breathe air, and walk away to live on land!

* The **giant anteater's** snout is *so* long that it has to be balanced by an equally long tail—to keep the anteater from falling over as it shuffles along on its knuckles, sniffing out tasty ants and termites.

* **Dolphins** are very intelligent and "talk" to each other across wide watery distances with a huge variety of sounds. These swift, sleek swimmers have a highly-developed navigational sense and roam the seas without ever getting lost. Dolphins are playful, funny, and helpful, too—they look after weak or injured dolphins and will guide frightened and exhausted human swimmers safely back to shore.

* *And finally . . . the ultimate astronauts —jellyfish in space!*

In 1991 the scientists at NASA sent 2,700 appropriately-named **moon jellyfish** on a nine-day shuttle mission

* *Toothy tongues!*

Abelone snails are very peculiar —their bodies inside the shell are just muscular "feet" with a head at one end and long tongue filled with teeth!

to outer space. The jellies were part of an experiment to study the effects of weightlessness.

But the jellies took the honor in their stride. After all, they have always been pioneers—600 million years ago jellyfish were the first animals to develop nerve cells.

5. Funny Fish

The one and only . . . anglerfish!

Anglerfish live deep, deep down in the dark undersea waters. With their black bodies hidden in the murky gloom, they stay quiet and still—waving a thin, luminous fishing rod gently to and fro in front of their massive tooth-filled jaws—just waiting to catch an unwary victim.

The tiny male anglerfish is so much smaller than the huge female that, when mating, he bites into her side and mingles his blood stream with hers, before he shrivels away. *This pair truly become one fish!*

* Some **parrotfish** just can't make up their minds—and change their beautiful colours three times during their lives.

* Clever little **clownfish** protect themselves from bigger fish by living among the dangerous stinging tentacles of **sea anemones**—rather like avoiding the frying pan by jumping into the fire. And yet they remain unharmed.

The clownfish prepare themselves by rubbing against the stings, a little more each time, until they are well used to their exciting new homes. In return, they keep the anemone clean—which is only fair!

* A **flounder** is *so* flat that both of its eyes are on the same side of its body!

* *Never step on a stonefish!*

Good advice, because the grotesque **stonefish** has thirteen sharp dorsal spikes which carry a strong, excruciatingly painful, and often fatal, poison.

But this unpleasant predator is hard to spot. It can camouflage itself perfectly—*when lying absolutely still, it looks exactly like a slime-covered rock!*

* **Mudskippers** can breathe in air as well as water and, when tides are low, they become "walking fish" and crawl around in the mud on their two leglike front fins—while checking for danger with their revolving eyes, which they hold above the water even when swimming.

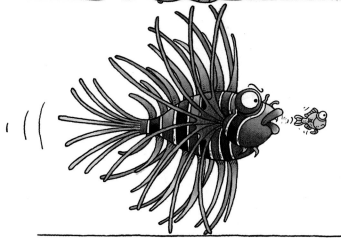

* **Lionfish** are also poisonous and with their striped bodies, waving fins, and spiny manes, they sweep through tropical seas hunting down smaller prey. Lionfish are not, however, as sporting as their namesakes, for they hunt in packs herding their victims into corners before gobbling them up.

* **seahorses** glide through the water with their heads held high like miniature warhorses, elegant and dignified—propelled by swiftly beating dorsal fins.

Seahorse fathers are among the world's best—they carry the eggs in a special stomach pouch and give birth to the young seahorses.

6. Hide and Seek

* The **chameleon** is the most famous of all the animal disguisers—altering its own body color to match new surroundings, or to reflect a change of mood!

    But during the mating season, male chameleons simply let go completely, conjuring up the brightest, loudest, and most noticeable colors imaginable to attract a mate and discourage rivals. Nothing that a Paris fashion show can offer is as outrageous as a chameleon's "catwalk of colors."

* **Chameleons** are also noted for the length of their tongues. Tucking itself inconspicuously among a group of nicely-matching leaves, the chameleon waits patiently until a suitable victim comes within range—then, ZAP!, out shoots its sticky-ended tongue which is longer than its body and tail put together! When it's not in use, the chameleon's tongue folds neatly into place like a narrow venetian blind.

* **Crab spiders,** which look just like small, bulbous crabs, also change color to match the flowers on which they sit, waiting for prey. They become yellow, white, mauve, or pastel pink—but these soft colors mask the truly nasty nature of these little carnivores.

    While the unfairly-nicknamed **black widow spider** usually *doesn't* eat her partner after mating, the female crab spider certainly does —*unless he first takes the precaution of tying her legs to the ground with silk!*

Some animals will disguise themselves as just about anything for safety . . .

Brown butterflies use a pattern of eyespots on their wings to fool hungry birds. When a bird dives down to attack, it may be frightened away by the "eyes" of a much larger animal or peck just the spotted wing—leaving the butterfly's body unharmed.

* Hide that shadow!
Butterflies fold their wings vertically —unlike **moths** whose wings fold horizontally. When facing the sun, the butterfly's shadow becomes the thinnest of lines.

* **Leaf insects** sit swaying in the wind like fresh green leaves, while their legs masquerade as crumpled, torn edges. Later in the year, you can see—or rather not see—**lappet moths** and **leaf frogs** the colors of dead brown leaves.

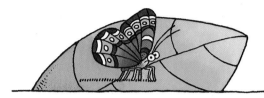

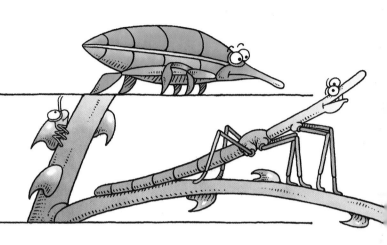

* **Tree-hoppers** look like thorns, while **stick insects** are almost indistinguishable from twigs.

* Both **zebras** and **tigers** use their striped coats as camouflage as they move among a background of slender trees and long waving grass. Stripes break up the shape of an animal —moving or still—and make it hard to see. So the zebra can hide from hunters and the tiger sneak up close to its prey. A standoff? Not at all—*the zebras live in the African bush, while the tigers hunt in the jungles of Asia.*

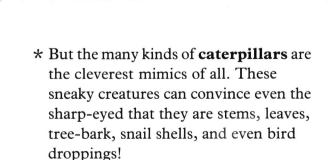

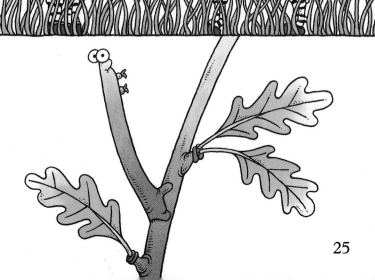

* But the many kinds of **caterpillars** are the cleverest mimics of all. These sneaky creatures can convince even the sharp-eyed that they are stems, leaves, tree-bark, snail shells, and even bird droppings!

7. How the Other Half Lives . . .

* The **water spider** spins itself a "diving bell" of silk which traps enough air bubbles to enable this little air-breathing spider to live underwater.

* Nature's best imitator isn't, in fact, a **parrot** or **mynah bird**—talented as these two chatterers are—but the gray and white **mockingbird** of North America. This talented mocker can imitate almost any sound—from the calls of other birds, insects, frogs and other animals to the sound of a fire siren, a rusty gate, or an alarm clock! Its repertoire has been enjoyed for centuries; it plays a part in Native American mythology as the bringer of language and is called *Cencontlatolly*, the bird of 400 tongues.

* **Elephants** certainly deserve their reputation for intelligence—they can send low-frequency greetings across miles of open bushland, show affection and love, and mourn their dead. Elephants dig salt from the earth, remember where to find water in the desert and use their truly remarkable trunks (with 100,000 different muscles) to do almost anything—*from lifting a heavy log to picking up a feather*.

* **Gorillas** are strong and tall, broad-chested and powerful. They look so ferocious that they make perfect film monsters—but it's all an act. Gorillas are peaceful vegetarians who like to play with their children and snooze in leafy nests at night!

* When it comes to strength and endurance, however, the true strongman of the animal world are —**beetles**! For sheer power relative to its size and weight the mighty beetle leaves huge **elephants** and muscular **gorillas** far behind.

  They are pretty big, too. **Goliath beetles** are *the largest insects in the world*—more than 5 inches long, 3 inches wide and weighing more than 3½ ounces.

* Male **stag beetles** stage serious slow motion fights. Like heavily armored gladiators they lock their huge jaws (which jut out like antlers) and hang on—grimly pushing and pulling. Suddenly, one of these insect sumo wrestlers bites his opponent, throws him over his shoulder, and dashes him to the ground with a loud "clack." Honor is satisfied.

* American "tumblebugs" are **dung beetles**. As their names suggests, these large beetles make large balls of dung which they push up hills and down with great perseverence and strength.

  Dung beetles are members of the same family as the sacred **scarab beetle** of ancient Egypt—preserved in glittering jewels and worshipped as an image of the sun god, Ra.

  It was one of these large scarabs which was reported by a scientist to have set a record for strength in 1955 —by lifting a load 850 times its own weight!

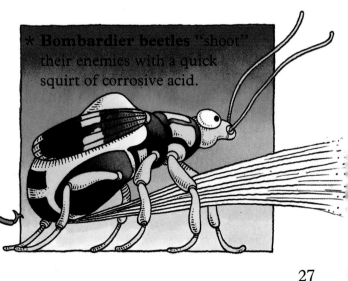

* **Bombardier beetles** "shoot" their enemies with a quick squirt of corrosive acid.

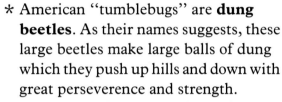

27

* The saucer-eyed **African bush baby** acts as a sort of large furry **honeybee** by pollinating flowers as it feeds. Moving among the flowers of the Baobab trees, this odd little mammal carries pollen on its furry nose. But, unlike bees, the busy bush baby works only at night —during the day they rest, huddling together high in the tree like—well rather like a swarm of bees!

* *Have basket, will travel!*

And speaking of pollinating—the hardworking **honeybees** have devised a simple and effective way to direct other honeybees to a good patch of nectar-filled flowers—by dancing. When the lucky explorer gets back to the hive she executes a complicated waggle dance which tells the other worker bees exactly how to reach the flowers. Then off they buzz to collect the sweet nectar and fill the little pollen baskets on their legs.

* The bumbling **bumble bee** flies at a relatively slow speed of 11.2 miles per hour, but even that is more than the busily toiling honeybee which can only manage a little over 7 miles per hour as it buzzes along looking for food. But slow and steady is obviously successful for the worker bees travel great distances and carry back large amounts of nectar—as much as 5 pounds in total weight—to a single hive each day!

---

* *Introducing—the world's most successful insects!*

Bees are great co-operators, but even they must bow to **ants** as the most social of all insects. Ants *never* live alone but always share their lives in very well-organized colonies. Ant colonies have full employment with each individual ant doing a special job: there are ants who clean, ants who farm, and ants who build. Soldier ants stand guard while the queen does nothing but lay eggs.

* **Ants** are clever engineers and build many different kinds of nests: **weaver ants** glue the edges of leaves together to make pouches; **tropical ants** build nests out of chewed wood pulp high up in trees; **wood ants** erect huge, many-

nests out of chewed wood pulp high up in trees; **wood ants** erect huge, many-

* **Leaf-cutter ants** snip off large pieces from leaves and flowers with their sharp jaws and carry them home on their backs—each ant with its colorful burden moving carefully along in single file.

roomed underground nests linked by a network of tunnels housing thousands of ants in one enormous colony. These patient builders bring every single grain of earth back up to the surface as they carry on the work of building and repairing the nest and its tunnels. These ant mounds are thatched with twigs which keep the nests warm and cozy—with windows which are opened in summer and stopped up with leaves to keep out winter drafts.

* **African army ants** have no homes but march together in their millions across the forest floor—creating a blanket of moving black bodies. When they reach a gap, the first wave of ants lock their legs together to form a living bridge and the remaining mass crosses safely to other side.

Nothing gets in their way! These ferocious ants will devour any other animal they find in their path—*no matter how large.*

* But not all **ants** are carnivorous; some prefer fruit, flowers, nectar, and the honeydew created by other nectar-feeding insects—especially **aphids**. Ants just love honeydew, and to make sure they get enough, they "milk" it from the aphids, by stroking them —*just

But ants may have the last laugh, and when humans are as extinct as dinosaurs, these efficient and highly co-operative ceatures will still be marching and building, farming and chewing, and generally organizing a world that belongs to . . . insects!

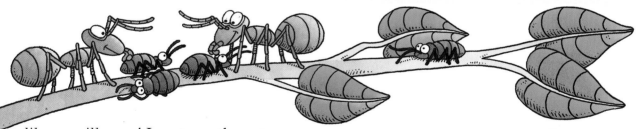

like we milk cows!* In return, the ants protect the aphids from **ladybugs**, who like the aphids better than the honeydew.

But in harsh desert climates, ants need to gather all the food they can find and store it. **Honeypot ants** in Australia store the honeydew in their own bodies—which grow bigger and bigger—*until they can't move at all!* Then, all through the dryest months these "living larders" feed the rest of the colony with golden drops of honeydew until they are empty again.

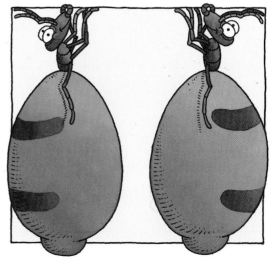

Animal Index

Abelone snails 21
African bush baby 28
Albatross 8
Anteater 21
Ants: 28, 29
  African army ants 29
  Honeypot ants 29
  Leaf-cutter ants 28
  Tropical ants 28
  Weaver ants 28
  Wood ant 28
Aphids 29
Arrow-poison frogs 19
Aurochs 16
Axolotls 20

Basilisk 17
Basilisk lizard 17
Bees 28
Beetles: 27
  Bombardier beetles 27
  Dung beetles 27
  Goliath beetles 27
  Scarab beetle 27
  Stag beetles 27
Black widow spider 24
Blue whale 10, 15
Brown butterflies 24
Bulls 14, 15
Bumble bee 28
Butterflies 25

Caterpillars 25
Centipede 20
Cerberus 14

Chameleon 24
Chimera 14
Common housefly 13
Coyote 11
Crab spiders 24
Crabs 18
Crocodile 9, 16, 17
Dinosaurs: 7, 8, 9
  Archaeopteryx 8, 20
  Brachiosaurus 7
  Brontosaurus 7
  Diplodocus 7
  Ichthyosaur 9
  Phobosuchus 9
  Pteranodon 8
  Pterosaur 8
  Stegasaurus 8
  Tyrannosaurus Rex 8
Dolphins 21
Dragons 16, 17
Dugongs 15

Eagles 14
Elephants 10, 26, 27
Elephant bird 9

Falcons 14
Fish: 22, 23
  Anglerfish 22
  Clownfish 22
  Flounder 22
  Lionfish 23
  Mudskipper 23
  Parrotfish 22
  Stonefish 23